INDUSTRIALIZATION

EXAMPLES FROM THE EUROPEAN EXPERIENCE

1789-1914

A brief essay

*Elena Scarfagna Rossi*

2018©Elena Scarfagna Rossi

ISBN: 9781719865791

First publication January 1996, Hull University

esrwriter@gmail.com

Independent publication

All rights reserved

The term "industrialization" refers to the system of economic and socio-political changes that reflected the shift from the manufacture system, based on manual labour, to large scale machine industry.

Industrialisation began with the invention and application of machinery for production and culminated in the production of machines by machines. As a result, the capitalist mode of production emerged victorious in its struggle against the feudal mode of production.

The historical preconditions for the development of large scale machine industry were created by the manufacture form of capitalistic production. The primitive accumulation of capital assured the further development of capitalist relations through the creation of an army of people deprived of their means of livelihood whose only commodity was their labour power and through the accumulation of large financial resources used by the rising class of capitalists to acquire means of production and labour power. The increase of capitalist production inevitably led to the rapid expansion of both domestic and foreign markets. The bourgeoisie's efforts to accelerate capital accumulation were impeded by the limitation of manufacturers, which were based on artisan techniques.

Industrialisation was a general historical phenomenon that characterized a stage in the development of capitalism in the industry of several countries. However, the gradual development of the prerequisites for the shift from manufactures to large-scale machine industry varied from country to country.

Industrialisation began in Great Britain in the 1760s after the English Civil War of the 17th century had cleared the way for the development of capitalist relations. Manufacture production had reached its peak in England, and the Dutch manufactures had fallen far behind the English ones. According to Marx, the narrow technological basis of manufacture production came into conflict with the requirement of production that manufacture itself had created. This conflict was most acute in the cotton industry, since the demand for cotton was increasing very rapidly.

The shift from artisan or manufacture production to machine production began with a change in the means of labour. In the 1770s and 1780s a mechanical spindle called the jenny, invented by J. Hargreaves, came into use and subsequently the spinning mule, invented by Crompton in the 1770s, was introduced. Once the spindles had been widely adopted, all cotton thread and yarn were produced in factories.

The mechanisation of one industry necessitated an increase in labour productivity in other industries as well. The improvement of production techniques in cotton spinning created a disproportion between spinning and weaving. The incorporation of new weaving techniques in turn speeded up the mechanisation of cloth printing dyeing, and other industries. The spread of machine technology led to the decline of cottage industry and to the impoverishment of numerous small producers.

The rapid growth of industrial output and expanding markets required improvements on transportation. Steamships and steam locomotives came into use in the first quarter of the 19th century.

The rapid spread of machine technology came into conflict with the artisan techniques by which machines were produced. One of the most acute and long-lasting disproportions that arose during industrialisation was the discrepancy between the rapidly growing demand for new means of labour and the limitations of the manufacture production of machines. This discrepancy was resolved through the large-scale use of machines to build machines. The mechanisation of various industries and the differentiation in mechanical implements of labour created the conditions for the shift from the simple cooperation of machines to machine systems, the basic and most essential characteristic of large-scale machine industry.

Between 1810 and 1830 large-scale machine industry completely replaced manufacture and artisan production in Great Britain, which became an important industrial power. The rapid growth of productive forces was accompanied by an equally rapid intensification of the contradiction in the capitalist mode of production. The first economic crisis of overproduction occurred in Great Britain in 1825.

France, Germany, and other nations followed Great Britain on the road of large-scale industry.

In Italy the industrial revolution began in the 1840s. Factory production developed mainly in northern Italy, and this only intensified the economic backwardness of the south. Large-scale machine industry completely supplanted cottage industry and manufacture production in the last third of the 19th century.

The French Revolution played a decisive role in speeding up the development of capitalist relations in France by destroying the feudal order. In the 1780s the first steps were taken to mechanise cotton spinning, but many decades passed before manufacture production gave way to machine systems in other leading industries.

The shift from manufacture to large-scale machine industry came much later in Germany, where the dominance of feudal and semi-feudal relations hindered the development of capitalist industry.

The development of large-scale machine industry in these countries accelerated sharply after the Revolutions of 1848-49. In Germany, the final stage of industrial revolution, which came in the late1850s and 1860s, was marked by a rapid growth of the heavy industry.

The shift from manufacture to large-scale machine industry introduced radical changes not only into the technical basis of production but also into the sphere of social relations. In his description of industrial revolution, Lenin stressed that it meant an abrupt and profound transformation of all social relations. The success of industrialisation in the leading branches of production created the material prerequisites for the further rapid development of productive forces. In addition to making industry the main branch of social production, industrialisation also brought about its complete separation from agriculture and the rapid growth of large industrial centres.

The development of industrialisation inevitably led to the breakdown of the closed world of the patriarchal system and increased population mobility. The capitalist use of machine technology, however, increased the exploitation of hired workers and transformed large enterprises into prison factories and the worker into an appendage of the machine. The growth of factory production intensified the contradictions between intellectual and physical labour, as well as between town and country. The further mechanisation of production led to the expulsion of part of the labour force from the factory, creating mass unemployment. The contradiction between the social nature of production and the private form of appropriation caused world-wide economic overproduction crises.

The victory of factory system marked the final split between the various groups participating in production and increased class differentiation. Industrialisation culminated in the formation of the two main classes of capitalist society, the proletariat and the bourgeoisie. As industrialisation grew, the number of factory workers increased. Moreover, the factory transformed them into permanent wage workers, thereby shaping the proletariat into an independent class. Reduced to despair by the monstrous exploitation in the late 18th and the early 19th centuries, the English workers sometimes protested by destroying machines, which they considered the cause of their misery. As large-scale machine industry and the class-consciousness of workers developed, the proletariat engaged in more advanced and organised forms of struggle against the system of capitalist exploitation. The working class combined methods of economic struggle with active political campaigns. A mass political revolutionary movement of the proletariat, known as Chartism, developed in Great Britain in the 1830s and 1840s. During this period the first large-scale insurrections of the working class broke out in France and Germany.

In Russia the real industrialisation began in the first half of the 19th century. The transition from manufactures to factories first occurred in the cotton industry, later spreading to other industries. The replacement of manual labour by machines sharply raised labour productivity and entailed a great leap forward in the development of productive forces. However, the development of industrialisation required many free hired workers, an extensive market for industrial products, and the flow of large amounts of capital into production. The creation of these conditions was inhibited by the existence of serfdom. Therefore, the shift from manufactures to factories in the pre-Reform period further intensified the crisis of the feudal system and hastened the downfall of serfdom.

In pre-Reform Russia, only the cotton industry, the sugar beet refining industry, and the paper industry produced most of their output in factories. In other leading industries the shift from manual labour to machines was basically completed in the late 1870s and the early 1880s. Permanent wageworkers had already existed in Russia during the time of serfdom. They were not yet proletarians, since most them were not free. Only the abolition of serfdom transformed the permanent wageworkers of the pre-Reform period into real proletarians.

The proletariat developed rapidly after the Peasant Reform of 1861. It included industrial workers from the period of serfdom, landless peasant or peasant with insufficient work, and peasant who had been ruined during social differentiation. The shift from manufactures to factories was the decisive stage in the formation of the bourgeoisie as a class.

During industrialisation through all Europe intellectuals and philosophers were assaulting economic abuses, old unjust privileges, misgovernment, and intolerance. Their ideas, which carried a new emphasis on the worth of individual, helped to disregard for long the welfare of the common man. In some countries, such as France and Germany, the school reformers had to combat the prevailing notion that free schools were to be provided only for pauper children, if at all. The new economic changes called upon the schools, public and private, to broaden their aims and curricula. Schools were expected to prepare children for jobs and for individual development and success.

During the first industrial revolution, especially in Northern Europe, France, Northern Italy and the West side of Russia, widening gaps between rich and poor, the growth of large-scale industry and its dependence on science and technological advancement, had big effects on educational systems. Development of industry brought about a tremendous demand for secondary and higher education. Education tended to reach not only the higher classes, the bourgeoisie, but even the middle and low classes through a state education system.

# BIBLIOGRAPHY

## Books

- Aldcroft D., Ville S.P., (eds.), The European Economy 1750-1914: A Thematic Approach, (Manchester: Manchester University Press, 1994)

- Berlanstein L.R., (ed.), The Industrial Revolution and Work in Nineteenth-century Europe, (London: Routledge,1992)

- Goodman J., Honeyman K., Gainful Pursuits: The Making of Industrial Europe 1600-1914, (London: Edward Arnold, 1988)

- Marx K., Capital: A Critique of Political Economy, vol. I., (Harmondsworth: Penguin, 1976)

## Miscellaneous Sources

- *History of Education* in Britannica Encyclopedia, vol.18, (Chicago: University of Chicago, 1990)

- *Industrial Revolution* in Great Soviet Encyclopedia, vol.21, (New York: Macmillan, 1978)

www.ingramcontent.com/pod-product-compliance
Lightning Source LLC
Chambersburg PA
CBHW031524210526
45464CB00007B/3018